The Night Before Christmas

Clement C. Moore

Jody Wheeler

IDEALS CHILDREN'S BOOKS

Nashville, Tennessee

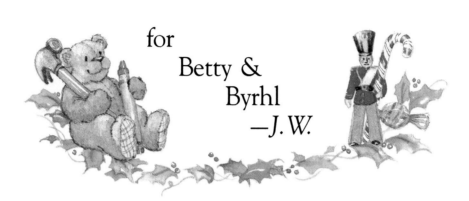

for
Betty &
Byrhl
—*J.W.*

'T was the night before Christmas,
when all through the house
Not a creature was stirring, not even a mouse.
The stockings were hung by the chimney with care
In hopes that Saint Nicholas soon would be there.

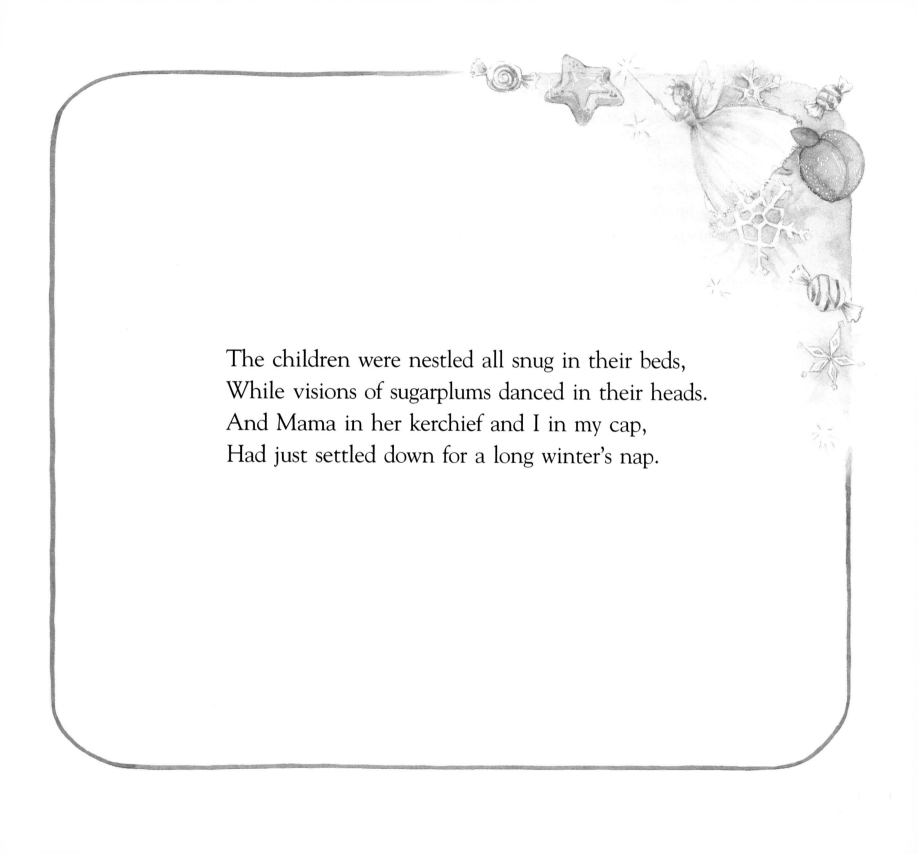

The children were nestled all snug in their beds,
While visions of sugarplums danced in their heads.
And Mama in her kerchief and I in my cap,
Had just settled down for a long winter's nap.

When out on the lawn there arose such a clatter,
I sprang from my bed to see what was the matter.
Away to the window I flew like a flash,
Tore open the shutters and threw up the sash.

The moon on the breast of the new-fallen snow
Gave a luster of midday to objects below.
When, what to my wondering eyes should appear,
But a miniature sleigh and eight tiny reindeer,
With a little old driver so lively and quick,
I knew in a moment it must be Saint Nick.

More rapid than eagles his coursers they came,
And he whistled and shouted and called them by name:
"Now, Dasher! Now, Dancer! Now, Prancer and Vixen!
On, Comet! On, Cupid! On, Donder and Blitzen!
To the top of the porch, to the top of the wall!
Now, dash away! Dash away! Dash away, all!"

As dry leaves that before the wild hurricane fly,
When they meet with an obstacle, mount to
  the sky,
So up to the housetop the coursers they flew
With a sleigh full of toys and Saint Nicholas too,

And then in a twinkling I heard on the roof
The prancing and pawing of each little hoof.
As I drew in my head and was turning around,
Down the chimney Saint Nicholas came with a bound.

He was dressed all in fur from his head to his foot,
And his clothes were all tarnished with ashes and soot.
A bundle of toys he had flung on his back,
And he looked like a peddler just opening his pack.
His eyes—how they twinkled! His dimples—how merry!
His cheeks were like roses, his nose like a cherry!
His droll little mouth was drawn up like a bow,
And the beard on his chin was as white as the snow.
The stump of a pipe he held tight in his teeth,
And the smoke it encircled his head like a wreath.

He had a broad face and a little round belly
That shook when he laughed like a bowl full of jelly.
He was chubby and plump, a right jolly old elf,
And I laughed when I saw him in spite of myself.
A wink of his eye and a twist of his head
Soon gave me to know I had nothing to dread.
He spoke not a word, but went straight to his work,
And filled all the stockings; then turned with a jerk,
And laying his finger aside of his nose
And giving a nod, up the chimney he rose;

He sprang to his sleigh, to his team gave a whistle,
And away they all flew like the down of a thistle.
But I heard him exclaim ere he drove out of sight,

"Happy Christmas to all and to all a good night!"

About the Poem

This classic poem was written in 1822 by Dr. Clement C. Moore, professor of Oriental literature in New York and father of nine children. On Christmas Eve, Dr. Moore returned home from a trip to town with the concept for the poem and intended to present it as a very special gift to his six-year-old daughter, Charity.

Charity memorized the poem, then recited it to a family friend who, in turn, shared it with her Sunday School class. The next Christmas, the poem, originally entitled "A Visit from St. Nicholas," appeared in the *Sentinel* of Troy, New York, its author anonymous.

Moore, a modest man, was embarrassed by the notoriety of the poem. Not until 1837 did he reluctantly acknowledge himself as author. Clement Moore's habits and lifestyle continued relatively unchanged for the remainder of his life, but his poem lives on in the hearts of children and adults who delight in the Christmas joy they find every time they read it.